LIFE
Lessons
WITH MAX LUCADO

BOOK OF GALATIANS

FREE IN CHRIST

D1025344

MAX LUCADO

Prepared by
THE LIVINGSTONE CORPORATION

Published by
THOMAS NELSON™
Since 1798

www.thomasnelson.com

LIFE
Lessons
WITH MAX LUCADO

CONTENTS

HOW TO STUDY THE BIBLE

This is a peculiar book you are holding. Words crafted in another language. Deeds done in a distant era. Events recorded in a far-off land. Counsel offered to a foreign people. This is a peculiar book.

It's surprising that anyone reads it. It's too old. Some of its writings date back five thousand years. It's too bizarre. The book speaks of incredible floods, fires, earthquakes, and people with supernatural abilities. It's too radical. The Bible calls for undying devotion to a carpenter who called himself God's Son.

Logic says this book shouldn't survive. Too old, too bizarre, too radical.

The Bible has been banned, burned, scoffed, and ridiculed. Scholars have mocked it as foolish. Kings have branded it as illegal. A thousand times over, the grave has been dug and the dirge has begun, but somehow the Bible never stays in the grave. Not only has it survived; it has thrived. It is the single most popular book in all of history. It has been the best-selling book in the world for years!

There is no way on earth to explain it. Which perhaps is the only explanation. The answer? The Bible's durability is not found on earth; it is found in heaven. For the millions who have tested its claims and claimed its promises, there is but one answer: the Bible is God's book and God's voice.

As you read it, you would be wise to give some thought to two questions. What is the purpose of the Bible? and How do I study the Bible? Time spent reflecting on these two issues will greatly enhance your Bible study.

What is the purpose of the Bible?

Let the Bible itself answer that question.

Since you were a child you have known the Holy Scriptures which are able to make you wise. And that wisdom leads to salvation through faith in Christ Jesus. (2 Tim. 3:15 NCV)

The purpose of the Bible? Salvation. God's highest passion is to get his children home. His book, the Bible, describes his plan of salvation. The purpose of the Bible is to proclaim God's plan and passion to save his children.

That is the reason this book has endured through the centuries. It dares to tackle the toughest questions about life: Where do I go after I die? Is there a God? What do I do with my fears? The Bible offers answers to these crucial questions. It is the treasure map that leads us to God's highest treasure, eternal life.

But how do we use the Bible? Countless copies of Scripture sit unread on bookshelves and nightstands simply because people don't know how to read it. What can we do to make the Bible real in our lives?

The clearest answer is found in the words of Jesus. He promised:

Ask, and God will give to you. Search, and you will find. Knock, and the door will open for you. (Matt. 7:7 NCV)

The first step in understanding the Bible is asking God to help us. We should read prayerfully. If anyone understands God's Word, it is because of God and not the reader.

But the Helper will teach you everything and will cause you to remember all that I told you. The Helper is the Holy Spirit whom the Father will send in my name. (John 14:26 NCV)

Before reading the Bible, pray. Invite God to speak to you. Don't go to Scripture looking for your idea; go searching for his.

Not only should we read the Bible prayerfully; we should read it carefully. *Search and you will find* is the pledge. The Bible is not a newspaper to be skimmed but rather a mine to be quarried.

Search for it like silver, and hunt for it like hidden treasure. Then you will understand respect for the LORD, and you will find that you know God. (Prov. 2:4–5 NCV)

Any worthy find requires effort. The Bible is no exception. To understand the Bible you don't have to be brilliant, but you must be willing to roll up your sleeves and search.

Be a worker who is not ashamed and who uses the true teaching in the right way. (2 Tim. 2:15 NCV)

Here's a practical point. Study the Bible a bit at a time. Hunger is not satisfied by eating twenty-one meals in one sitting once a week. The body needs a steady diet to remain strong. So does the soul. When God sent food to his people in the wilderness, he didn't provide loaves already made. Instead, he sent them manna in the shape of *"thin flakes like frost . . . on the desert ground"* (Ex. 16:14 NCV).

God gave manna in limited portions. God sends spiritual food the same way. He opens the heavens with just enough nutrients for today's hunger. He provides *"a command here, a command there. A rule here, a rule there. A little lesson here, a little lesson there"* (Isa. 28:10 NCV).

Don't be discouraged if your reading reaps a small harvest. Some days a lesser portion is all that is needed. What is important is to search every day for that day's message. A steady diet of God's Word over a lifetime builds a healthy soul and mind.

A little girl returned from her first day at school. Her mom asked, "Did you learn anything?"

"Apparently not enough," the girl responded, "I have to go back tomorrow and the next day and the next . . ."

Such is the case with learning. And such is the case with Bible study. Understanding comes little by little over a lifetime.

There is a third step in understanding the Bible. After the asking and seeking comes the knocking. After you ask and search, then knock.

Knock, and the door will open for you. (Matt. 7:7 NCV)

To knock is to stand at God's door. To make yourself available. To climb the steps, cross the porch, stand at the doorway, and volunteer. Knocking goes beyond the realm of thinking and into the realm of acting.

To knock is to ask, What can I do? How can I obey? Where can I go?

It's one thing to know what to do. It's another to do it. But for those who do it, those who choose to obey, a special reward awaits them.

The truly happy are those who carefully study God's perfect law that makes people free, and they continue to study it. They do not forget what they heard, but they obey what God's teaching says. Those who do this will be made happy. (James 1:25 NCV)

What a promise. Happiness comes to those who do what they read! It's the same with medicine. If you only read the label but ignore the pills, it won't help. It's the same with food. If you only read the recipe but never cook, you won't be fed. And it's the same with the Bible. If you only read the words but never obey, you'll never know the joy God has promised.

Ask. Search. Knock. Simple, isn't it? Why don't you give it a try? If you do, you'll see why you are holding the most remarkable book in history.

INTRODUCTION TO THE BOOK OF GALATIANS

All the Emancipation Proclamation lacked was the president's signature. But Abraham Lincoln was not ready. His hand was sore from greeting visitors at a reception.

"Let me wait until my hand is better," he reportedly requested. "I don't want my signature to be shaky. I want people to know I set the slaves free in confidence."

The book of Galatians is the Emancipation Proclamation for the church. Written by one who had known slavery, it declares and defines Christian liberty. Paul wrote it to refute the devilish idea that salvation is based on adherence to a religious code.

Many of the early Christians were Jewish Christians who were accustomed to following the Law. Though they had accepted the gift of grace offered by Christ on the cross, some were falling away—substituting human effort for God's gift. Paul recognized this for what it was—legalism.

Everywhere the gospel has been preached, there have been those who contend that it is too good to be true. Faith isn't enough, argues the legalist. We must earn God's approval. Some teach that we earn God's favor by what we know (intellectualism). Others insist we are saved by what we do (moralism). Still others claim that salvation is determined by what we feel (emotionalism).

However you package it, Paul contests, legalism is heresy. Salvation comes only through the cross—no additions, no alterations.

We are free in Christ. *"We have freedom now, because Christ made us free. So stand strong. Do not change and go back into the slavery of the law"* (5:1 NCV). Galatians is a document of freedom. As you read, note the confidence of the writer. His hand doesn't shake; his conviction doesn't waver.

Neither should ours.

LESSON ONE

LEAVING GRACE?

MAX
LUCADO

REFLECTION

Not very many people enjoy confrontation. Few go through their days looking to pick a fight. And yet, conflict is an unavoidable fact of life. Describe your feelings and your usual course of action when it is obvious that you have to speak hard truths to a friend, neighbor, or colleague.

SITUATION

Having preached the good news of God's amazing grace across Galatia (i.e., modern-day Turkey), the apostle Paul was greatly troubled to hear that some influential religious teachers in that region were insisting that salvation is *not* by grace alone. He wrote to refute this idea that God's favor is earned by keeping Jewish laws and customs.

OBSERVATION

Read Galatians 1:1–9 from the NCV or the NKJV.

NCV

¹From Paul, an apostle. I was not chosen to be an apostle by human beings, nor was I sent from human beings. I was made an apostle through Jesus Christ and God the Father who raised Jesus from the dead. ²This letter is also from all those of God's family who are with me.

To the churches in Galatia:

³Grace and peace to you from God our Father and the Lord Jesus Christ. ⁴Jesus gave himself for our sins to free us from this evil world we live in, as God the Father planned. ⁵The glory belongs to God forever and ever. Amen.

⁶God, by his grace through Christ, called you to become his people. So I am amazed that you are turning away so quickly and believing something different than the Good News. ⁷Really, there is no other Good News. But some people are confusing you; they want to change the Good News of Christ. ⁸We preached to you the Good News. So if we ourselves, or even an angel from heaven, should preach to you something different, we should be judged guilty! ⁹I said this before, and now I say it again: You have already accepted the Good News. If anyone is preaching something different to you, he should be judged guilty!

NKJV

¹Paul, an apostle (not from men nor through man, but through Jesus Christ and God the Father who raised Him from the dead), ²and all the brethren who are with me,

To the churches of Galatia:

³Grace to you and peace from God the Father and our Lord Jesus Christ, ⁴who gave Himself for our sins, that He might deliver us from this present evil age, according to the will of our God and Father, ⁵to whom be glory forever and ever. Amen.

⁶I marvel that you are turning away so soon from Him who called you in the grace of Christ, to a different gospel, ⁷which is not another; but there are some who trouble you and want to pervert the gospel of Christ. ⁸But even if we, or an angel from heaven, preach any other gospel to you than what we have preached to you, let him be accursed. ⁹As we have said before, so now I say again, if anyone preaches any other gospel to you than what you have received, let him be accursed.

EXPLORATION

1. The first few sentences of Paul's letter to the Galatians have an abrupt and somber feel. Why?

2. Paul starts out by presenting his "credentials," so to speak. Why do we feel the need to do this, and when is this act valid or invalid?

3. Why is the "new" gospel the Galatians are embracing *not* good news (v. 7)?

4. The word "accursed" (vv. 8–9 NKJV) means "eternally condemned." What does this suggest about tinkering with the gospel or altering Christ's message?

5. What is the simple gospel? (Hint: see 1 Corinthians 15:1–4.)

INSPIRATION

"What is the work [God] wants us to do? Pray more? Give more? Study? Travel? Memorize the Torah? What is the work he wants?" Sly is this scheme of Satan. Rather than lead us away from grace, he causes us to question grace or to earn it . . . and in the end we never even know it.

What is it, then, that God wants us to do? What is the work he seeks? Just believe. Believe the One he sent. *"The work God wants you to do is this: Believe the One he sent"* (John 6:29 NCV).

Someone is reading this and shaking his or her head and asking, "Are you saying it is possible to go to heaven with no good works?" The answer is no. Good works are a requirement. Someone else is reading and asking, "Are you saying it is possible to go to heaven without good character?" My answer again is no. Good character is also required. In order to enter heaven one must have good works and good character.

But, alas, there is the problem. You have neither.

Oh, you've done some nice things in your life. But you do not have enough good works to go to heaven regardless of your sacrifice. No matter how noble your gifts, they are not enough to get you into heaven.

Nor do you have enough character to go to heaven. Please don't be offended. (Then again, be offended, if necessary.) You're probably a very decent person. But decency isn't enough. Those who see God are not the decent; they are the holy. *"Anyone whose life is not holy will never see the Lord"* (Heb. 12:14 NCV).

You may be decent. You may pay taxes and kiss your kids and sleep with a clean conscience. But apart from Christ you aren't holy. So how can you go to heaven?

Only believe.

Accept the work already done, the work of Jesus on the cross.

Only believe . . .

It's that simple? It's that simple. It's that easy? There was nothing easy at all about it. The cross was heavy, the blood was real, and the price was extravagant. It would have bankrupted you or me, so he paid it for us. Call it simple. Call it a gift. But don't call it easy.

Call it what it is. Call it grace. (From *A Gentle Thunder* by Max Lucado)

REACTION

6. Why is it so hard for people to grasp the concept of grace?

7. What are some of the things (other than Christ) that Christians rely on to try to establish their approval in God's sight?

8. How would you answer the person who read this passage and said, "I don't get why Paul is so upset over a few theological semantics?"

9. When you look at your church, do any trends "amaze" you or cause you to "marvel" (in a negative sense)?

10. Is the gospel message you share with others marked by radical and risky-sounding grace?

11. How will you respond the next time you hear someone share a distorted version of the gospel?

LIFE LESSONS

Grace is what sets Christianity apart from every religion in the world. God's unearnable salvation, forgiveness, and eternal life offered, not as a reward, but as free gifts. Nothing—absolutely nothing—required on our part, except to believe. No fine print and no strings attached. When we trust in what Christ has done, when we rely solely on his promises, all the treasures of heaven are ours. It doesn't matter how miserably you've failed in the past. It's irrelevant how messed up your life is right now. Grace is true and certain no matter what you might do or fail to do in the future. It sounds too good to be true, doesn't it? But that, in a nutshell, is the simple gospel. The only question is this: Have you received Christ's remarkable gift?

DEVOTION

Father, thank you for the gospel. I could never earn your favor, but I can be a recipient of grace. I can enjoy all your blessings simply by trusting in Christ as my all-sufficent Savior. Help me to live this message. Help me to show it by my life and share it with my lips.

For more Bible passages on the gospel of grace, see Acts 15:11; 20:24; Romans 3:22–24; and Titus 3:4–7.

To complete the book of Galatians during this twelve-part study, read Galatians 1:1–9.

JOURNALING

When were you first struck by the "free" nature of the gospel—that faith, not works, is the doorway to peace with God?

LESSON TWO

DEFENDING
THE GOSPEL

MAX
LUCADO

REFLECTION

In one sense, life is all about our interaction with God. Some are running from him. Others are ignoring him. That person caught a glimpse of God in a friend's life and now wants to take a closer look. This person wandered away from the faith of their childhood and now is on the road back. What's your unique faith story?

SITUATION

False teachers had infiltrated the Galatian church, attempting to add legalistic requirements to the simple gospel. Paul reiterated the truth of salvation—that it is only by faith in Christ alone—by sharing the story of his own miraculous conversion.

OBSERVATION

Read Galatians 1:11–24 from the NCV or the NKJV.

NCV

11Brothers and sisters, I want you to know that the Good News I preached to you was not made up by human beings. 12I did not get it from humans, nor did anyone teach it to me, but Jesus Christ showed it to me.

13You have heard about my past life in the Jewish religion. I attacked the church of God and tried to destroy it. 14I was becoming a leader in the Jewish religion, doing better than most other Jews of my age. I tried harder than anyone else to follow the teachings handed down by our ancestors.

15But God had special plans for me and set me apart for his work even before I was born. He called me through his grace 16and showed his son to me so that I might tell the Good News about him to those who are not Jewish. When God called me, I did not get advice or help from any person. 17I did not go to Jerusalem to see those who were apostles before I was. But, without waiting, I went away to Arabia and later went back to Damascus.

18After three years I went to Jerusalem to meet Peter and stayed with him for fifteen days. 19I met no other apostles, except James, the brother of the Lord. 20God knows that these things I write are not lies. 21Later, I went to the areas of Syria and Cilicia.

22In Judea the churches in Christ had never met me. 23They had only heard it said, "This man who was attacking us is now preaching the same faith that he once tried to destroy." 24And these believers praised God because of me.

NKJV

11But I make known to you, brethren, that the gospel which was preached by me is not according to man. 12For I neither received it from man, nor was I taught it, but it came through the revelation of Jesus Christ.

13For you have heard of my former conduct in Judaism, how I persecuted the church of God beyond measure and tried to destroy it. 14And I advanced in Judaism beyond many of my contemporaries in my own nation, being more exceedingly zealous for the traditions of my fathers.

15But when it pleased God, who separated me from my mother's womb and called me through His grace, 16to reveal His Son in me, that I might preach Him among the Gentiles, I did not immediately confer with flesh and blood, 17nor did I go up to Jerusalem to those who were apostles before me; but I went to Arabia, and returned again to Damascus.

18Then after three years I went up to Jerusalem to see Peter, and remained with him fifteen days. 19But I saw none of the other apostles except James, the Lord's brother. 20(Now concerning the things which I write to you, indeed, before God, I do not lie.)

21Afterward I went into the regions of Syria and Cilicia. 22And I was unknown by face to the churches of Judea which were in Christ. 23But they were hearing only, "He who formerly persecuted us now preaches the faith which he once tried to destroy." 24And they glorified God in me.

EXPLORATION

1. When did Christ first become real to you—more than just a name or an idea?

2. Why was Paul an "unlikely" candidate for becoming a Christian, much less God's number one missionary? (See Acts 9:1–20.)

3. Why does Paul make such a big deal about not getting advice or help from any person after his conversion?

4. Why do people get so fanatical about religion? How can we tell when zeal and passion cross over the line into fanaticism?

5. What does Paul's testimony here (especially v. 15) reveal about God's patience and mercy?

INSPIRATION

Though God's people often forgot their God, God didn't forget them. He kept his word . . .

God didn't give up. He never gives up.

When Joseph was dropped into a pit by his own brothers, God didn't give up.

When Moses said, "Here I am, send Aaron," God didn't give up.

When the delivered Israelites wanted Egyptian slavery instead of milk and honey, God didn't give up.

When Aaron was making a false god at the very moment Moses was with the true God, God didn't give up.

When only two of the ten spies thought the Creator was powerful enough to deliver the created, God didn't give up.

When Samson whispered to Delilah, when Saul roared after David, when David schemed against Uriah, God didn't give up.

When God's word lay forgotten and man's idols stood glistening, God didn't give up.

When the children of Israel were taken into captivity, God didn't give up.

He could have given up. He could have turned his back. He could have walked away from the wretched mess, but he didn't.

He didn't give up.

When he became flesh and was the victim of an assassination attempt before he was two years old, he didn't give up.

When the people from his own hometown tried to push him over a cliff, he didn't give up.

When his brothers ridiculed him, he didn't give up.

When he was accused of blaspheming God by people who didn't fear God, he didn't give up.

When Peter worshiped him at the supper and cursed him at the fire, he didn't give up.

When people spat in his face, he didn't spit back. When the bystanders slapped him, he didn't slap them. When a whip ripped his sides, he didn't turn and command the awaiting angels to stuff that whip down that soldier's throat.

And when human hands fastened the divine hands to a cross with spikes, it wasn't the soldiers who held the hands of Jesus steady. It was God who held them steady. (From *Six Hours One Friday* by Max Lucado)

REACTION

6. What situations in your own life are proof that God doesn't give up on his children?

7. What features of the Christian faith indicate that it obviously wasn't fabricated by humans?

8. How zealous are you? If you've lost your passion for Christ, how can you get it back?

9. Scholars believe that Paul's time in Arabia (v. 17) was a time of study, reflection, and preparation. How, realistically, can we find time for reflection in the midst of our busy lives?

10. Paul emphasizes here how his experience with the Lord was direct and not mediated secondhand through other people. How much of your knowledge of God is based on first-person experience?

11. Paul's conversion resulted in a dramatic transformation that had everyone buzzing. What have been the most significant changes in your life since you met Christ?

LIFE LESSONS

It's often said, "The Lord works in mysterious ways." How true. Start with the gospel of grace. The enemies of God being offered unconditional pardon and adoption into the royal family of God? Heaven's most glorious riches lavished on the least deserving? It all reads like a fairy tale. And it gets even wilder. God announces his intention to partner with the likes of us so others can experience his love and grace. He could use angels or employ some other supernatural means. Instead he uses us. And what do we do? Mostly we stumble and fall and fail. Yet the Lord never gives up on us and never aborts his plan. He works in us and through us, despite us. The villains become the heroes. What a mystery! What a miracle! What a God we serve!

DEVOTION

Father, you amaze me! Thank you for the beauty and power of the gospel. I open my heart to you and invite you to work in me. Transform me. Make my life a continual tribute to your goodness and grace.

For more Bible passages on zeal, see Psalm 119:139; Ecclesiastes 9:10; John 2:17; 4:34; Acts 18:25; Romans 9:3; 10:1; 1 Corinthians 9:22; 14:12; and 2 Timothy 1:6.

To complete the book of Galatians during this twelve-part study, read Galatians 1:10—2:10.

JOURNALING

Write out the story of your own journey to faith.

RIGHT
WITH GOD

MAX
LUCADO

REFLECTION

Just about every religious tradition or church group has its own code of conduct. What were some of the activities, both prescribed and prohibited, by the spiritual community in which you grew up?

SITUATION

The non-Jewish Galatians had put their faith in Christ, but were subsequently being told that they must adhere to Jewish laws to insure God's approval. The apostle Peter added to the confusion by showing favoritism to the Jews. Paul confronted and corrected Peter and reiterated that only Jesus can make us right with God.

OBSERVATION

Read Galatians 2:11–21 from the NCV or the NKJV.

NCV

11When Peter came to Antioch, I challenged him to his face, because he was wrong.
12Peter ate with the non-Jewish people until some Jewish people sent from James came
to Antioch. When they arrived, Peter stopped eating with those who weren't Jewish, and
he separated himself from them. He was afraid of the Jews. 13So Peter was a hypocrite,
as were the other Jewish believers who joined with him. Even Barnabas was influenced
by what these Jewish believers did. 14When I saw they were not following the truth of
the Good News, I spoke to Peter in front of them all. I said, "Peter, you are a Jew, but
you are not living like a Jew. You are living like those who are not Jewish. So why do
you now try to force those who are not Jewish to live like Jews?"

15We were not born as non-Jewish "sinners," but as Jews. 16Yet we know that a person
is made right with God not by following the law, but by trusting in Jesus Christ. So we,
too, have put our faith in Christ Jesus, that we might be made right with God because
we trusted in Christ. It is not because we followed the law, because no one can be made
right with God by following the law.

17We Jews came to Christ, trying to be made right with God, and it became clear that
we are sinners, too. Does this mean that Christ encourages sin? No! 18But I would really
be wrong to begin teaching again those things that I gave up. 19It was the law that put
me to death, and I died to the law so that I can now live for God. 20I was put to death
on the cross with Christ, and I do not live anymore—it is Christ who lives in me. I still
live in my body, but I live by faith in the Son of God who loved me and gave himself to
save me. 21By saying these things I am not going against God's grace. Just the opposite, if
the law could make us right with God, then Christ's death would be useless.

NKJV

11Now when Peter had come to Antioch, I withstood him to his face, because he was to
be blamed; 12for before certain men came from James, he would eat with the Gentiles;
but when they came, he withdrew and separated himself, fearing those who were of the
circumcision. 13And the rest of the Jews also played the hypocrite with him, so that even
Barnabas was carried away with their hypocrisy.

14But when I saw that they were not straightforward about the truth of the gospel, I said
to Peter before them all, "If you, being a Jew, live in the manner of Gentiles and not as
the Jews, why do you compel Gentiles to live as Jews? 15We who are Jews by nature, and
not sinners of the Gentiles, 16knowing that a man is not justified by the works of the
law but by faith in Jesus Christ, even we have believed in Christ Jesus, that we might be
justified by faith in Christ and not by the works of the law; for by the works of the law
no flesh shall be justified.

17"But if, while we seek to be justified by Christ, we ourselves also are found sinners, is Christ therefore a minister of sin? Certainly not! 18For if I build again those things which I destroyed, I make myself a transgressor. 19For I through the law died to the law that I might live to God. 20I have been crucified with Christ; it is no longer I who live, but Christ lives in me; and the life which I now live in the flesh I live by faith in the Son of God, who loved me and gave Himself for me. 21I do not set aside the grace of God; for if righteousness comes through the law, then Christ died in vain."

EXPLORATION

1. What was Peter doing that warranted Paul's accusing him of hypocrisy?

2. What are some similar ways modern believers are guilty of presenting a distorted picture of the gospel of grace?

3. When should a Christian confront another Christian privately, and when should such disagreements be handled publicly?

4. What does "justified" (found three times in v. 16 in the NKJV) mean?

5. There have always been those who feel that "too much emphasis on grace" encourages people to believe that they can live however they want. Is this a valid concern?

INSPIRATION

Jesus did for us what I did for one of my daughters in the shop at New York's La Guardia Airport. The sign above the ceramic pieces read Do Not Touch. But the wanting was stronger than the warning, and she touched. And it fell. By the time I looked up, ten-year-old Sara was holding the two pieces of a New York City skyline. Next to her was an unhappy store manager. Over them both was the written rule. Between them hung a nervous silence. My daughter had no money. The manager had no mercy. So I did what dads do. I stepped in. "How much do *we* owe you?" I asked.

How was it that I owed anything? Simple. She was my daughter. And since she could not pay, I did.

Since you and I cannot pay, Christ did. We've broken so much more than souvenirs. We've broken commandments, promises, and worst of all, we've broken God's heart.

But Christ sees our plight. With the law and the wall and shattered commandments on the floor, he steps near (like a neighbor) and offers a gift (like a Savior).

What do we owe? We owe God a perfect life. Perfect obedience to every command. Not just the command of baptism, but the commands of humility, honesty, integrity. We can't deliver. Might as well charge us for the property of Manhattan. But Christ can and he did. (From *Next Door Savior* by Max Lucado)

REACTION

6. Why do so many people have a hard time understanding and embracing Christ's actions on their behalf?

7. If Paul hadn't spoken out against Peter's inconsistent behavior, what might have happened?

8. Under what circumstances would or should you stand up against an influential spiritual leader?

9. What are some ways you see modern believers living by rules rather than living by faith?

10. What would you tell a friend who inquired, "If salvation is a free gift, and it is based on what Christ has already done for me, why does it matter how I live?"

11. Describe what Galatians 2:20 will look like as you try to live it out in your life tomorrow.

LIFE LESSONS

Trying to get right with God by keeping a bunch of religious rules is a formula for frustration and failure. First problem, whose rules? Such requirements vary from religion to religion, person to person, and generation to generation. What if you're working from the wrong list? Second problem, how do we define what it means to "keep" those rules? Do we have to follow them perfectly? Or are we allowed a reasonable number of mistakes and missteps? And what is considered "reasonable"? The gospel of Christ eliminates all this confusion by stating categorically that no one but Christ is good enough. Only through faith in him, only by relying on his efforts on our behalf, do we qualify for heaven.

DEVOTION

Father, we are not made right with you by human efforts, and we do not stay right with you by works. Remaining "in your good graces" means counting on Christ alone to live in us.

For more Bible passages on salvation by grace, see Romans 5:15; 11:6; Ephesians 2:4–10; and Titus 2:11.

To complete the book of Galatians during this twelve-part study, read Galatians 2:11–21.

JOURNALING

Looking over your usual patterns of living, what specific behaviors could be considered (1) legalistic, (2) abusive of God's unending grace, and (3) demonstrating true freedom in Christ?

L E S S O N   F O U R

FAITH
ALONE!

MAX
LUCADO

REFLECTION

Faith is one of those words that we use a lot but probably don't demonstrate as we should. It ought to be a verb, really, something we actively *do*. But in our language it's a noun, just one more good character quality to try to possess. What are the true hallmarks of a person who has a living and active faith?

SITUATION

With urgency and intensity, the apostle Paul admonishes the believers in Galatia to remember the fundamental truth of Christianity: Just as we came to Christ by faith alone, so now we also walk with him by faith alone. Religious works, no matter how great, do not merit greater approval from God.

OBSERVATION

Read Galatians 3:1–9 from the NCV or the NKJV.

NCV

1You people in Galatia were told very clearly about the death of Jesus Christ on the cross. But you were foolish; you let someone trick you. 2Tell me this one thing: How did you receive the Holy Spirit? Did you receive the Spirit by following the law? No, you received the Spirit because you heard the Good News and believed it. 3You began your life in Christ by the Spirit. Now are you trying to make it complete by your own power? That is foolish. 4Were all your experiences wasted? I hope not! 5Does God give you the Spirit and work miracles among you because you follow the law? No, he does these things because you heard the Good News and believed it.

⁶*The Scriptures say the same thing about Abraham: "Abraham believed God, and God accepted Abraham's faith, and that faith made him right with God." ⁷So you should know that the true children of Abraham are those who have faith. ⁸The Scriptures, telling what would happen in the future, said that God would make the non-Jewish people right through their faith. This Good News was told to Abraham beforehand, as the Scripture says: "All nations will be blessed through you." ⁹So all who believe as Abraham believed are blessed just as Abraham was.*

NKJV

¹*O foolish Galatians! Who has bewitched you that you should not obey the truth, before whose eyes Jesus Christ was clearly portrayed among you as crucified? ²This only I want to learn from you: Did you receive the Spirit by the works of the law, or by the hearing of faith?— ³Are you so foolish? Having begun in the Spirit, are you now being made perfect by the flesh? ⁴Have you suffered so many things in vain—if indeed it was in vain?*

⁵*Therefore He who supplies the Spirit to you and works miracles among you, does He do it by the works of the law, or by the hearing of faith? ⁶just as Abraham "believed God, and it was accounted to him for righteousness." ⁷Therefore know that only those who are of faith are sons of Abraham. ⁸And the Scripture, foreseeing that God would justify the Gentiles by faith, preached the gospel to Abraham beforehand, saying, "In you all the nations shall be blessed." ⁹So then those who are of faith are blessed with believing Abraham.*

EXPLORATION

1. Why did Paul use such strong language and tone in his letter to the Galatians?

2. What role does the Spirit of God play in our conversion and ultimate transformation?

3. What are some specific ways Christians can inhibit the Spirit's work in their lives?

4. What is Paul's reason for mentioning Abraham, the Old Testament saint?

5. Paul distinguishes between a life that is reliant upon the Holy Spirit and one that depends largely on human effort. Practically speaking, what's the difference?

INSPIRATION

The real question is not, how do I get more of the Spirit? But rather, how can you, Spirit, have more of me? We'd expect a Mother Teresa-size answer to that question. Build an orphanage. Memorize Leviticus. Bathe lepers. Stay awake through a dozen Lucado books. *Do this and be filled,* we think.

"Do this on your own and be tired," God corrects. Do you desire God's Spirit? Here is what you do. Ask. "Everyone who asks will receive . . . You know how to give good things to your children. How much more your heavenly Father will give the Holy Spirit to those who ask him!" (Luke 11:10, 13 NCV).

The Spirit fills as prayers flow. Desire to be filled with strength? Of course you do. Then pray, "Lord, I receive your energy. Empowered by your Holy Spirit, I can do all things through Christ, who gives me strength." Welcome the Spirit into every room of your heart.

I did something similar with the air of my air conditioner. As I study in my dining room, cool air surrounds me. Outside the sidewalk sizzles in brick-oven heat. But inside I'm as cool as the other side of the pillow. Why? Two reasons. A compressor sits next to my house. I did not build nor install it. It came with the mortgage. Credit the cool house on a good compressor.

But equally credit the open vents. I did not install the "air makers," but I did open the "air blockers." Cool air fills the house because vents are open. I went from room to room, lowering the levers and releasing the air. The Holy Spirit will fill your life as you do the same: as you, room by room, invite him to flow in.

Try this: before you climb out of bed, mentally escort the Spirit into every room of your house. Before your feet touch the floor, open each vent. Got anger in a bedroom? Unpayable bills on a desk? Conflicts in an office? Need some air in the cellar or a change of atmosphere in the hallways? Invite him to fill each corridor of your life. (From *Come Thirsty* by Max Lucado)

REACTION

6. How do you know when you're filled with the Spirit of God?

7. When was the last time an older, wiser Christian challenged you bluntly to re-think a spiritual idea or practice in your life?

8. How can a Christian tell when he or she has stopped living by faith and started relying on "the flesh" (v. 3 NKJV)?

9. In what ways are you like Abraham?

10. Why does Satan work so hard to obscure the gospel? How has he distorted it in our time?

11. Can you think of some specific ways you can open your life to God's Spirit?

LIFE LESSONS

Just like Abraham, we are made right with God by faith alone. And just like Abraham, we are commissioned to bless all nations by sharing and showing the good news of God's forgiveness. God's intention is for us—now forgiven and free—to be bright beacons of hope and life in the world. But when we forget that salvation is by grace, we stop shining. Living in our own strength darkens our hearts and deadens our enthusiasm. What's more, when we fall into the trap of trying to earn God's approval, we paint a misleading and unattractive picture of what it means to be a child of God. Revel in the astonishing good news that you are—now, already—fully accepted in Christ. Then spend your life revealing that amazing grace to others.

DEVOTION

O Lord, keep me from being tricked. Protect me from the foolish belief that I can do anything to warrant your continued approval. Show me how to live freely and fully in the grace of your Spirit.

For more Bible passages on legalism, see Mark 2:24; Luke 6:2; 13:14; John 5:10; Acts 15:5; 16:3; 21:20; 22:3; Romans 10:2; and Galatians 1:14.

To complete the book of Galatians during this twelve-part study, read Galatians 3:1–9.

JOURNALING

Using Galatians 5:22–23 as a standard, evaluate your own walk of faith.

LESSON FIVE

THE LAW
AND THE
PROMISE

MAX
LUCADO

REFLECTION

When it comes to faith, some people are extremely serious—almost to the point of being grim. Others take a more breezy and light-hearted approach. The more serious group spends much time looking back (or looking within); the light-hearted folks more commonly look forward. The former tend to err on the side of legalism, the latter on the side of license. Which end of the spectrum do you tend to gravitate toward?

SITUATION

The apostle Paul is instructing the Galatian Christians not to listen to false teachers urging them to surrender the freedom they have in Christ for bondage to the Jewish law. Here he shows why religious rules are incapable of helping a person become right with God and why only Christ is able to save us.

OBSERVATION

Read Galatians 3:10—18 from the NCV or the NKJV.

NCV

¹⁰But those who depend on following the law to make them right are under a curse, because the Scriptures say, "Anyone will be cursed who does not always obey what is written in the Book of the Law." ¹¹Now it is clear that no one can be made right with God by the law, because the Scriptures say, "Those who are right with God will live by trusting in him." ¹²The law is not based on faith. It says, "A person who obeys these things will live because of them." ¹³Christ took away the curse the law put on us. He changed places with us and put himself under that curse. It is written in the Scriptures, "Anyone whose body is displayed on a tree is cursed." ¹⁴Christ did this so that God's blessing promised to Abraham might come through Jesus Christ to those who are not Jews. Jesus died so that by our believing we could receive the Spirit that God promised.

¹⁵Brothers and sisters, let us think in human terms: Even an agreement made between two persons is firm. After that agreement is accepted by both people, no one can stop it or add anything to it. ¹⁶God made promises both to Abraham and to his descendant. God did not say, "and to your descendants." That would mean many people. But God said, "and to your descendant." That means only one person; that person is Christ. ¹⁷This is what I mean: God had an agreement with Abraham and promised to keep it. The law, which came four hundred thirty years later, cannot change that agreement and so destroy God's promise to Abraham. ¹⁸If the law could give us Abraham's blessing, then the promise would not be necessary. But that is not possible, because God freely gave his blessings to Abraham through the promise he had made.

NKJV

¹⁰For as many as are of the works of the law are under the curse; for it is written, "Cursed is everyone who does not continue in all things which are written in the book of the law, to do them." ¹¹But that no one is justified by the law in the sight of God is evident, for "the just shall live by faith." ¹²Yet the law is not of faith, but "the man who does them shall live by them."

¹³Christ has redeemed us from the curse of the law, having become a curse for us (for it is written, "Cursed is everyone who hangs on a tree"), ¹⁴that the blessing of Abraham might come upon the Gentiles in Christ Jesus, that we might receive the promise of the Spirit through faith.

¹⁵Brethren, I speak in the manner of men: Though it is only a man's covenant, yet if it is confirmed, no one annuls or adds to it. ¹⁶Now to Abraham and his Seed were the promises made. He does not say, "And to seeds," as of many, but as of one, "And to your Seed," who is Christ. ¹⁷And this I say, that the law, which was four hundred and thirty years later, cannot annul the covenant that was confirmed before by God in Christ, that it should make the promise of no effect. ¹⁸For if the inheritance is of the law, it is no longer of promise; but God gave it to Abraham by promise.

EXPLORATION

1. Why would Paul describe those whose spirituality consists of "religious rule following" as being under a curse?

2. But what about that rare person who demonstrates radical devotion to God, who lives selflessly, who is never seen doing anything wrong? Doesn't that count for something in God's sight?

3. "The just shall live by faith" (v. 11 NKJV)—what does this important biblical statement really mean?

4. Some of the false teachers in Galatia were apparently claiming that the law given to Moses was the fulfillment of the promise given to Abraham. How does Paul refute that idea?

5. Why were the law-keeping Pharisees so confused and so antagonistic to Christ?

INSPIRATION

I have a sketch of Jesus laughing. It hangs on the wall across from my desk.

It's quite a drawing. His head is back. His mouth is open. His eyes are sparkling. He isn't just grinning. He isn't just chuckling. He's roaring. He hasn't heard or seen one like that in quite a while. He's having trouble catching his breath.

It was given to me by an Episcopal priest who carries cigars in his pocket and collects portraits of Jesus smiling. "I give them to anyone who might be inclined to take God too seriously," he explained as he handed me the gift.

He pegged me well.

I'm not one who easily envisions a smiling God. A weeping God, yes. An angry God, OK. A mighty God, you bet. But a chuckling God? It seems too . . . too . . . too unlike what God should do—and be. Which just shows how much I know—or don't know—about God.

What do I think he was doing when he stretched the neck of the giraffe? An exercise in engineering? What do I think he had in mind when he told the ostrich where to put his head? Spelunking? What do I think he was doing when he designed the mating call of an ape? Or the eight legs of the octopus? And what do I envision on his face when he saw Adam's first glance at Eve? A yawn?

Hardly.

As my vision improves and I'm able to read without my stained glasses, I'm seeing that a sense of humor is perhaps the only way God has put up with us for so long.

Is that him with a smile as Moses does a double take at the burning bush that speaks?

Is he smiling again as Jonah lands on the beach, dripping gastric juices and smelling like whale breath?

Is that a twinkle in his eye as he watches the disciples feed thousands with one boy's lunch?

Do you think that his face is deadpan as he speaks about the man with a two-by-four in his eye who points out a speck in a friend's eye?

Can you honestly imagine Jesus bouncing children on his knee with a somber face?

No, I think that Jesus smiled. I think that he smiled a bit at people and a lot with people. (From *In the Eye of the Storm* by Max Lucado)

REACTION

6. How does this image of a joy-filled Christ contrast with the somber, rule-keeping nature of many Christians?

7. "Anyone will be cursed who does not always obey what is written in the Book of the Law" (v. 10 NCV; also see James 2:10). Does this seem fair to you?

8. How does the good news of Christ "take the pressure off" believers?

9. List some of the spiritual blessings that are yours because Christ "changed places with us" (v. 13 NCV)?

10. How do you think you would have fared spiritually living as a devout Jew during Old Testament times?

11. What people in your sphere of influence think that being right with God depends on their living a good life? How can you help them see the truth of grace?

LIFE LESSONS

Wouldn't you love to have a video record of Jesus' meeting with Zaccheus (Luke 19:1–10)? The law-obsessed religious leaders looking on in shock as Jesus befriends a notorious crook. Bent on earning God's approval through their religious efforts, these Pharisees and scribes are harsh and judgmental. They frown a lot. They think they see, but in truth they are blind. They live in bondage to their own foolish pride. A few feet away stands Jesus, smiling, inviting himself to dinner. He is disarming and gracious. He offers unconditional freedom from the failures of the past, and a fresh start. Is there a better picture of life-giving grace? A grimmer illustration of the death that comes through trying to earn God's favor?

DEVOTION

Jesus, what a wonderful Savior you are! I thank you for putting yourself under the very curse meant for me. I praise you for blessing me with the gracious gift of eternal life. May I share this great promise and hope with all around me.

For more Bible passages on the law's inferiority, see Romans 3:19–20; 4:13–25; 8:3; Galatians 5:4–6; and Hebrews 3:1–6; 8:7–13.

To complete the book of Galatians during this twelve-part study, read Galatians 3:10–18.

JOURNALING

Before experiencing grace and understanding Christ's unconditional love, did you ever feel "cursed" spiritually?

LESSON SIX

THE PURPOSE
OF THE LAW

MAX
LUCADO

REFLECTION

We've all had the experience of trying to avoid certain temptations, such as hunting for hidden Christmas presents as kids, or as adults, resisting the offer of a fattening dessert. Explain the "forbidden fruit" syndrome—why does something that's off-limits seem to be all the more tempting?

SITUATION

If people are not saved by trying diligently to follow God's rules, then what is the purpose of all of those ancient laws? Paul answers this question in the following passage from his letter to the Galatians.

OBSERVATION

Read Galatians 3:19–29 from the NCV or the NKJV.

NCV

¹⁹So what was the law for? It was given to show that the wrong things people do are against God's will. And it continued until the special descendant, who had been promised, came. The law was given through angels who used Moses for a mediator to give the law to people. ²⁰But a mediator is not needed when there is only one side, and God is only one.

²¹Does this mean that the law is against God's promises? Never! That would be true only if the law could make us right. But God did not give a law that can bring life. ²²Instead, the Scriptures showed that the whole world is bound by sin. This was so the promise would be given through faith to people who believe in Jesus Christ.

²³Before this faith came, we were all held prisoners by the law. We had no freedom until God showed us the way of faith that was coming. ²⁴In other words, the law was our guardian leading us to Christ so that we could be made right with God through faith. ²⁵Now the way of faith has come, and we no longer live under a guardian.

²⁶⁻²⁷You were all baptized into Christ, and so you were all clothed with Christ. This means that you are all children of God through faith in Christ Jesus. ²⁸In Christ, there is no difference between Jew and Greek, slave and free person, male and female. You are all the same in Christ Jesus. ²⁹You belong to Christ, so you are Abraham's descendants. You will inherit all of God's blessings because of the promise God made to Abraham.

NKJV

¹⁹What purpose then does the law serve? It was added because of transgressions, till the Seed should come to whom the promise was made; and it was appointed through angels by the hand of a mediator. ²⁰Now a mediator does not mediate for one only, but God is one.

²¹Is the law then against the promises of God? Certainly not! For if there had been a law given which could have given life, truly righteousness would have been by the law. ²²But the Scripture has confined all under sin, that the promise by faith in Jesus Christ might be given to those who believe. ²³But before faith came, we were kept under guard by the law, kept for the faith which would afterward be revealed. ²⁴Therefore the law was our tutor to bring us to Christ, that we might be justified by faith. ²⁵But after faith has come, we are no longer under a tutor.

²⁶For you are all sons of God through faith in Christ Jesus. ²⁷For as many of you as were baptized into Christ have put on Christ. ²⁸There is neither Jew nor Greek, there is neither slave nor free, there is neither male nor female; for you are all one in Christ Jesus. ²⁹And if you are Christ's, then you are Abraham's seed, and heirs according to the promise.

EXPLORATION

1. Why can't we keep God's law?

2. If the law can't save us, why did God give it?

3. Legalism is the belief that following certain rules will make us more acceptable in God's sight. Why is this belief flawed?

4. Is God's law a good thing or a bad thing? Why?

5. What positive role does God's law play in our spiritual lives?

INSPIRATION

Remember the good ole' days when credit cards were imprinted by hand? The clerk would take your plastic and place it in the imprint machine, and *rrack-rrack,* the numbers would be registered and the purchase would be made . . .

If the noise didn't get you, the statement at the end of the month would. Thirty days is ample time to *rrack* up enough purchases to *rrack* your budget.

And a lifetime is enough to *rrack* up some major debt in heaven.

You yell at your kids, *rrack-rrack.*

You covet a friend's car, *rrack-rrack.*

You envy your neighbor's success, *rrack-rrack.*

You break a promise, *rrack-rrack.*

You lie, *rrack-rrack.*

You lose control, *rrack-rrack* . . .

Further and further in debt.

Initially, we attempt to repay what we owe . . . Every prayer is a check written, and each good deed is a payment made. If we can do one good act for every bad act, then won't our account balance out in the end? If I can counter my cussing with compliments, my lusts with loyalties, my complaints with contributions, my vices with victories—then won't my account be justified? . . .

There it is. That's the question. How do I deal with the debt I owe to God?

Deny it? My conscience won't let me.

Find worse sins in others? God won't fall for that.

Claim lineage immunity? Family pride won't help.

Try to pay it off? I could, but that takes us back to the problem. We don't know the cost of sin. We don't even know how much we owe.

Then what do we do? Listen to Paul's answer . . .

All need to be made right with God by his grace, which is a free gift. They need to be made free from sin through Jesus Christ. God gave him as a way to forgive sin through faith in the blood of Jesus. (Rom. 3:24–25 NCV)

Simply put: The cost of your sins is more than you can pay. The gift of your God is more than you can imagine. "A person is made right with God through faith," Paul explains, "not through obeying the law" (v. 28). (From *In the Grip of Grace* by Max Lucado)

REACTION

6. Why is it so difficult for people who are at least *mostly* moral to believe that they fall short of God's perfect standard (Rom. 3:23)?

7. How is the law of God a means to an end?

8. What's the value in reading and studying the Old Testament?

9. What does Paul mean when he calls the law our "guardian" (v. 24 NCV)?

10. If the law of God can't bring spiritual life (v. 21), where does spiritual life begin?

11. What "religious" habits or acts do you cling to, believing at some level that God likes you better or approves of you more when you do them?

LIFE LESSONS

In the time of Christ, the rule-keeping scribes had dissected and catalogued the Torah (the first five books of the Bible) into 613 individual commandments—365 "don'ts," and 248 "do's." Also on the scene were assorted rabbis (or teachers) who debated endlessly among themselves about how a God-fearing person was supposed to interpret and apply these divine decrees. Each rabbi had his own spin on things, his own "yoke" (way of understanding and living out the Torah) The result was a confusing, often contradictory, always exhausting way of life. Enter the rabbi Jesus. He offered a new "yoke" (see Matthew 11:28–30)—a radical new way of life that begins by "coming to him" (John 6:35, 37). This was Jesus' way of saying that we make peace with God and enter into real life, not when we try hard to be good, but when we trust Jesus to deal with our sins and give us his righteousness.

DEVOTION

Lord Jesus, thank you so much for giving me freedom in you. I praise you for the stunning fact that I am made right with God by grace, by trusting in your payment for my sins. You have written your law on my heart and given me your Spirit. Help me to listen to his voice and follow his lead.

For more Bible passages on the purpose of the law, see Romans 3:20; 5:20; 7:7; Ephesians 2:15; 1 Timothy 1:9; and Hebrews 7:19.

To complete the book of Galatians during this twelve-part study, read Galatians 3:19–29.

JOURNALING

Read Psalm 119 and record your impressions.

LESSON SEVEN

CHILDREN
OF GOD

MAX
LUCADO

REFLECTION

It is common to hear people make comments like, "Well, it doesn't matter whether you're Christian, Hindu, Muslim, whatever—the fact is we are *all* God's children." What do you think about this statement? Is it true, partly true, not true at all?

SITUATION

Paul is writing to the Christians in Galatia who are being told that being right with God requires, not merely faith in Christ, but also adherence to the Mosaic Law. He shows how the law was given only to point us to Christ. It cannot save us. Only through faith can we become true children of God.

OBSERVATION

Read Galatians 4:1–11 from the NCV or the NKJV.

NCV

¹I want to tell you this: While those who will inherit their fathers' property are still children, they are no different from slaves. It does not matter that the children own everything. ²While they are children, they must obey those who are chosen to care for them. But when the children reach the age set by their fathers, they are free. ³It is the same for us. We were once like children, slaves to the useless rules of this world. ⁴But when the right time came, God sent his Son who was born of a woman and lived under the law. ⁵God did this so he could buy freedom for those who were under the law and so we could become his children.

⁶Since you are God's children, God sent the Spirit of his Son into your hearts, and the Spirit cries out, "Father." ⁷So now you are not a slave; you are God's child, and God will give you the blessing he promised, because you are his child.

⁸In the past you did not know God. You were slaves to gods that were not real. ⁹But now you know the true God. Really, it is God who knows you. So why do you turn back to those weak and useless rules you followed before? Do you want to be slaves to those things again? ¹⁰You still follow teachings about special days, months, seasons, and years. ¹¹I am afraid for you, that my work for you has been wasted.

NKJV

¹Now I say that the heir, as long as he is a child, does not differ at all from a slave, though he is master of all, ²but is under guardians and stewards until the time appointed by the father. ³Even so we, when we were children, were in bondage under the elements of the world. ⁴But when the fullness of the time had come, God sent forth His Son, born of a woman, born under the law, ⁵to redeem those who were under the law, that we might receive the adoption as sons.

⁶And because you are sons, God has sent forth the Spirit of His Son into your hearts, crying out, "Abba, Father!" ⁷Therefore you are no longer a slave but a son, and if a son, then an heir of God through Christ.

⁸But then, indeed, when you did not know God, you served those which by nature are not gods. ⁹But now after you have known God, or rather are known by God, how is it that you turn again to the weak and beggarly elements, to which you desire again to be in bondage? ¹⁰You observe days and months and seasons and years. ¹¹I am afraid for you, lest I have labored for you in vain.

EXPLORATION

1. Reread 3:26–29 to review the context of this passage. What did Paul say about the Galatian Christians? Did he view them as "second-class" Christians?

2. What is Paul trying to say via his analogy of slaves and children?

3. What is meant by the statement that God "sent forth His Son . . . that we might receive the adoption as sons" (3:4–5 NKJV)?

4. What are the benefits of being in the family of God?

5. As "heirs" of God, what sort of inheritance do Christians stand to receive?

INSPIRATION

God is building a family. A permanent family. Earthly families enjoy short shelf lives. Even those that sidestep divorce are eventually divided by death. God's family, however, will outlive the universe. *"When I think of the wisdom and scope of his plan I fall on my knees and pray to the Father of all the great family of God—some of them already in heaven and some down here on earth"* (Eph. 3:14–15 TLB).

Jesus even defined his family according to faith, not flesh. *"A multitude was sitting around Him; and they said to Him, 'Look, Your mother and Your brothers are outside seeking You.' But He answered them, saying, 'Who is My mother, or My brothers? . . . Whoever does the will of God is My brother and My sister and mother'"* (Mark 3:32–33, 35 NKJV).

Common belief identifies members of God's family. And common affection unites them. Paul gives this relationship rule for the church: "Be devoted to one another in brotherly love" (Rom. 12:10 NIV). The apostle plays the word-smith here, bookending the verse with fraternal-twin terms. He begins with "philostorgos" ("philos" means friendly; "storgos" means family love) and concludes with "philadelphia" ("phileo" means tender affection; "adelphia" means brethren). An awkward but accurate translation of the verse might be "Have a friend/family devotion to each other in a friend/family sort of way." If Paul doesn't get us with the first adjective, he catches us with the second. In both he reminds us: the church is God's family.

You didn't pick me. I didn't pick you. You may not like me. I may not like you. But since God picked and likes us both, we are family.

And we treat each other as friends. (From *Cure for the Common Life* by Max Lucado)

REACTION

6. When has your church or circle of Christian friends felt most like a family?

7. How do cultural, racial, and socioeconomic differences make it difficult for Christians to live like a spiritual, close-knit family?

8. Paul says God sent Christ when the right time came (4:4 NCV). What made the first century the right time?

9. Do you address God as your "Father" (see 4:6)? Is this a tough concept to get your mind and heart around?

10. In your own faith journey right now, do you tend to live more like a slave of God's law or more like a child and heir of God?

11. What specifically needs to change for you to start treating other believers as spiritual siblings and fellow heirs of God?

LIFE LESSONS

What good parent loves one child more than another? None! However, a wise and caring dad will demonstrate his affection to his children in different ways. Depending on factors like personality and age and life situation, a mom will interact with her children in completely different ways. And so it is with God. He doesn't deal with his children exactly the same. Many realities come into play. And this is why we should never compare ourselves to others or envy another Christian's relationship with God. Each of our relationships with God will be unique. He will bless you in certain ways; he will bless another in different ways. Despite the discrepancies, we are each loved with his perfect, unconditional love. Each child adored and infinitely special. Each child an heir of endless spiritual blessings!

DEVOTION

Father, what a privilege to be your child through faith in Christ. Help me to remember today that I am a member of the ultimate royal family, and give me the wisdom and strength to live up to my pedigree.

For more Bible passages on God's children, see Isaiah 63:16; John 1:12; Romans 8:14; 2 Corinthians 6:18; Ephesians 5:8; Philippians 2:15; and 1 John 3:1.

To complete the book of Galatians during this twelve-part study, read Galatians 4:1–11.

JOURNALING

Do you think our view of God as our "Father" is strongly influenced by the kind of earthly father we have or had?

LESSON EIGHT

BECOMING
LIKE CHRIST

MAX
LUCADO

REFLECTION

"You can't teach an old dog new tricks," they say. "Once a child reaches the age of six, his or her personality is essentially set," the researchers declare. What do you think about these maxims? Do you know any dramatic exceptions to the notion that people can't change deeply and radically later in life?

SITUATION

Paul writes the Galatian Christians to reiterate the idea that salvation is by faith in God's promise, not adherence to God's law. He also stresses that God wants his children, by faith, to be transformed, to become like Christ in their thoughts, characters, and actions.

OBSERVATION

Read Galatians 4:12—20 from the NCV or the NKJV.

NCV

12Brothers and sisters, I became like you, so I beg you to become like me. You were very good to me before. 13You remember that it was because of an illness that I came to you the first time, preaching the Good News. 14Though my sickness was a trouble for you, you did not hate me or make me leave. But you welcomed me as an angel from God, as if I were Jesus Christ himself! 15You were very happy then, but where is that joy now? I am ready to testify that you would have taken out your eyes and given them to me if that were possible. 16Now am I your enemy because I tell you the truth?

17Those people are working hard to persuade you, but this is not good for you. They want to persuade you to turn against us and follow only them. 18It is good for people to show interest in you, but only if their purpose is good. This is always true, not just when I am with you. 19My little children, again I feel the pain of childbirth for you until you truly become like Christ. 20I wish I could be with you now and could change the way I am talking to you, because I do not know what to think about you.

NKJV

12Brethren, I urge you to become like me, for I became like you. You have not injured me at all. 13You know that because of physical infirmity I preached the gospel to you at the first. 14And my trial which was in my flesh you did not despise or reject, but you received me as an angel of God, even as Christ Jesus. 15What then was the blessing you enjoyed? For I bear you witness that, if possible, you would have plucked out your own eyes and given them to me. 16Have I therefore become your enemy because I tell you the truth?

17They zealously court you, but for no good; yes, they want to exclude you, that you may be zealous for them. 18But it is good to be zealous in a good thing always, and not only when I am present with you. 19My little children, for whom I labor in birth again until Christ is formed in you, 20I would like to be present with you now and to change my tone; for I have doubts about you.

EXPLORATION

1. What exactly does Paul mean when he speaks of becoming like other people (see 1 Corinthians 9:22)? How is this not being "fake"?

2. How had the Galatians' attitude and actions toward Paul changed?

3. How can truthfulness result in changed relationships—either good or bad?

4. How were the false teachers, the so-called Judaizers, in Galatia promoting a wrong kind of change?

5. What does it mean to have Christ "formed" in us (v. 19 NKJV)?

INSPIRATION

When my daughter Jenna was a toddler, I used to take her to a park not far from our apartment. One day as she was playing in a sandbox, an ice-cream salesman approached us. I purchased her a treat, and when I turned to give it to her, I saw her mouth was full of sand. Where I intended to put a delicacy, she had put dirt.

Did I love her with dirt in her mouth? Absolutely. Was she any less my daughter with dirt in her mouth? Of course not. Was I going to allow her to keep the dirt in her mouth? No way. I loved her right where she was, but I refused to leave her there. I carried her over to the water fountain and washed out her mouth. Why? Because I love her.

God does the same for us. He holds us over the fountain. "Spit out the dirt, honey," our Father urges. "I've got something better for you." And so he cleanses us of filth: immorality, dishonesty, prejudice, bitterness, greed. We don't enjoy the cleansing; sometimes we even opt for the dirt over the ice cream. "I can eat dirt if I want to!" we pout and proclaim. Which is true—we can. But if we do, the loss is ours. God has a better offer. He wants us to be just like Jesus.

Isn't that good news? You aren't stuck with today's personality. You aren't condemned to "grumpydom." You are tweakable. Even if you've worried each day of your life, you needn't worry the rest of your life. So what if you were born a bigot? You don't have to die one.

Where did we get the idea we can't change? From whence come statements such as, "It's just my nature to worry," or, "I'll always be pessimistic. I'm just that way," or "I have a bad temper. I can't help the way I react"? Who says? Would we make similar statements about our bodies? "It's just my nature to have a broken leg. I can't do anything about it." Of course not. If our bodies malfunction, we seek help. Shouldn't we do the same with our hearts? Shouldn't we seek aid for our sour attitudes? Can't we request treatment for our selfish tirades? Of course we can. Jesus can change our hearts. He wants us to have a heart like his. (From *Just Like Jesus* by Max Lucado)

REACTION

6. Jesus wants to change our hearts. What are the tools he uses to do this?

7. Why is change so difficult?

8. What forces or obstacles stand in the way of true, lasting soul transformation?

9. What does verse 16 reveal about human nature?

10. What are some specific areas in your life where you sense God has been trying to bring about deeper transformation?

11. How can you be a practical and positive force for change in the lives of those around you this week? Give some specific action steps.

LIFE LESSONS

The goal of the Christian life is not knowledge, comprehending a bunch of theology, or memorizing large chunks of the Bible. Following Christ is also not about activity, signing up to serve ceaselessly at church, or tackling a daily "to do" list for God. Christ's ultimate desire for each of us is to make us like himself. Once we become God's children by faith in Christ—once we receive a brand-new nature (see 2 Corinthians 5:17)—he wants to utterly transform, from the inside out, the way we think and talk and act. He does this primarily by the truth of his Word, by the power of his Spirit, and with the encouragement of his people. Life is his laboratory for remaking us into the people he originally envisioned, before sin plunged the world into darkness and ruin. Take heart, Christian, Christ is being formed in you!

DEVOTION

Father, thank you for the astounding promise that we will be changed. I pray that I might cooperate fully with the nudgings and promptings of your Spirit today. Give me eyes that see, and a will that yields to your sometimes painful transforming work.

For more Bible passages on transformation, see Romans 8:29; 1 Corinthians 15:49; 2 Corinthians 3:18; Philippians 3:21; 2 Peter 1:4; and 1 John 3:2.

To complete the book of Galatians during this twelve-part study, read Galatians 4:12–20.

JOURNALING

What are three character flaws that you would most like to change?

LESSON NINE

SLAVERY OR FREEDOM?

MAX
LUCADO

REFLECTION

There are so many great Old Testament Bible stories—Noah and the ark, the crossing of the Red Sea, David versus Goliath. What Old Testament story do you currently find to be most spiritually inspiring to you and why?

SITUATION

Under pressure from some persuasive false teachers, the church in Galatia was about to embrace an eclectic spirituality that mixed the grace of Christ with the law of Judaism. Paul used the Old Testament story of Sarah and Hagar (see Genesis 16) to illustrate the profound difference between living by law and living by grace.

OBSERVATION

Read Galatians 4:21–5:1 from the NCV or the NKJV.

NCV

21*Some of you still want to be under the law. Tell me, do you know what the law says?* 22*The Scriptures say that Abraham had two sons. The mother of one son was a slave woman, and the mother of the other son was a free woman.* 23*Abraham's son from the slave woman was born in the normal human way. But the son from the free woman was born because of the promise God made to Abraham.*

24*This story teaches something else: The two women are like the two agreements between God and his people. One agreement is the law that God made on Mount Sinai, and the people who are under this agreement are like slaves. The mother named Hagar is like that agreement.* 25*She is like Mount Sinai in Arabia and is a picture of the earthly Jewish city of Jerusalem. This city and its people, the Jews, are slaves to the law.* 26*But the heavenly Jerusalem, which is above, is like the free woman. She is our mother.* 27*It is written in the Scriptures:*

"Be happy, Jerusalem.

You are like a woman who never gave birth to children.

Start singing and shout for joy.

You never felt the pain of giving birth,

but you will have more children

than the woman who has a husband."

28My brothers and sisters, you are God's children because of his promise, as Isaac was then. 29The son who was born in the normal way treated the other son badly. It is the same today. 30But what does the Scripture say? "Throw out the slave woman and her son. The son of the slave woman should not inherit anything. The son of the free woman should receive it all." 31So, my brothers and sisters, we are not children of the slave woman, but of the free woman.

5:1We have freedom now, because Christ made us free. So stand strong. Do not change and go back into the slavery of the law.

NKJV

21Tell me, you who desire to be under the law, do you not hear the law? 22For it is written that Abraham had two sons: the one by a bondwoman, the other by a freewoman. 23But he who was of the bondwoman was born according to the flesh, and he of the freewoman through promise, 24which things are symbolic. For these are the two covenants: the one from Mount Sinai which gives birth to bondage, which is Hagar— 25for this Hagar is Mount Sinai in Arabia, and corresponds to Jerusalem which now is, and is in bondage with her children— 26but the Jerusalem above is free, which is the mother of us all. 27For it is written:

"Rejoice, O barren,

You who do not bear!

Break forth and shout,

You who are not in labor!

For the desolate has many more children

Than she who has a husband."

28Now we, brethren, as Isaac was, are children of promise. 29But, as he who was born according to the flesh then persecuted him who was born according to the Spirit, even so it is now. 30Nevertheless what does the Scripture say? "Cast out the bondwoman and her son, for the son of the bondwoman shall not be heir with the son of the freewoman." 31So then, brethren, we are not children of the bondwoman but of the free.

5:1Stand fast therefore in the liberty by which Christ has made us free, and do not be entangled again with a yoke of bondage.

EXPLORATION

1. What are the reasons some people prefer a law-based spirituality?

2. Review the basic story of Abraham, Sarah, Hagar, Isaac, and Ishamael (Genesis 15–17). Summarize what took place.

3. Why did Paul use this story to try to make a point with the Galatians?

4. How does living by the law result in bondage?

5. What does freedom in Christ really mean—in practical, everyday terms?

INSPIRATION

How would you fill in this blank?

A person is made right with God through _____ .

Simple statement. Yet don't let its brevity fool you. How you complete it is critical; it reflects the nature of your faith.

A person is made right with God through . . .

Being good. A person is made right with God through goodness. Pay your taxes. Give sandwiches to the poor. Don't drive too fast or drink too much or drink at all. Christian conduct—that's the secret.

Suffering. There's the answer. That's how to be made right with God—suffer. Sleep on dirt floors. Stalk through dank jungles. Malaria. Poverty. Cold days. Night-long vigils. Vows of chastity. Shaved heads, bare feet. The greater the pain, the greater the saint.

No, no, no. The way to be made right with God? Doctrine. Dead-center interpretation of the truth. Air-tight theology which explains every mystery. The Millennium simplified. Inspiration clarified. The role of women defined once and for all. God has to save us—we know more than he does.

How are we made right with God? All of the above are tried. All are taught. All are demonstrated. But none are from God.

In fact, that is the problem. None are from God. All are from people. Think about it. Who is the major force in the above examples? Humankind or God? Who does the saving, you or him?

If we are saved by good works, we don't need God—weekly reminders of the do's and don'ts will get us to heaven. If we are saved by suffering, we certainly don't need God. All we need is a whip and a chain and the gospel of guilt. If we are saved by doctrine then, for heaven's sake, let's study! We don't need God, we need a lexicon. Weigh the issues. Explore the options. Decipher the truth.

But be careful, student . . . if you are saving yourself, you never know for sure about anything. You never know if you've hurt enough, wept enough, or learned enough. Such is the result of computerized religion: fear, insecurity, instability. (From *And the Angels Were Silent* by Max Lucado)

REACTION

6. Describe the time in your life when the "lightbulb first came on," and you realized that the gospel offers unconditional, eternal acceptance and radical freedom?

7. What does the miraculous birth of Isaac suggest about the nature of grace?

8. What is the best way to respond to people who have a law-based approach to God?

9. In your own spiritual experience do you feel more often like a child of Hagar or like a child of Sarah? Why?

10. What are the most common ways you are tempted to fall back into thinking that approval with God is based on your compliance with certain rules? What rules?

11. How would you explain true Christian freedom to a teenager?

LIFE LESSONS

With the glorious freedom offered under God's *new* covenant, why would anyone prefer the old? It's a good question with a complex answer. Some don't like grace because it's too wild and risky. Others cringe because it's too vast and hard to measure. Still others bristle at grace because it's "unfair." Really bad people forgiven? Completely? Without *doing* anything? Opposite of grace stands the law. Hard and fast rules. Concrete formulas. Clear, measurable goals for which a person can strive. The law is a system that caters to human pride by promising to reward the hardest working, the most competitive. But the true reward? Bondage, a pervading sense of obligation, fear, and guilt. And—in fine print—the guarantee of ultimate failure. No wonder Paul says, "We have freedom now, because Christ made us free. So stand strong. Do not change and go back into the slavery of the law" (Gal. 5:1 NCV).

DEVOTION

Father, today when I am tormented by the ruthless demands and perfect standards of the law, remind me that I am, by virtue of Christ, free. I am a true spiritual child of Abraham and Sarah. Give me the wisdom and strength to cast away all such legalistic thoughts.

For more Bible passages on freedom in Christ, see Isaiah 61:1; John 8:32; Romans 6:18; 8:2, 21; 2 Corinthians 3:17; and Galatians 2:4.

To complete the book of Galatians during this twelve-part study, read Galatians 4:21–5:1.

JOURNALING

How is freedom from the law so unique to Christianity? In turn, how does this challenge you to live differently?

LESSON TEN

EMANCIPATION!

MAX
LUCADO

REFLECTION

Someone has wisely observed that life is both a journey and a battle. Indeed, both of these metaphors can be found in the Bible, descriptive of what it means and what it's like to try to follow Christ. Using the analogy of life as a journey, describe a recent experience in which you got off the path. What derailed you, and how did you get back on track?

SITUATION

To the Christians in Galatia who were being told that acceptance with God required them to not only believe in Jesus but also observe Jewish rituals, Paul writes this strong warning: It's not a "both-and" proposition. It's an "either-or" deal. You can try to keep the law (but you will have to do so perfectly); or you can acknowledge your need for Christ to be your substitute and Savior. There is no middle ground.

OBSERVATION

Read Galatians 5:2–15 from the NCV or the NKJV.

NCV

²Listen, I Paul tell you that if you go back to the law by being circumcised, Christ does you no good. ³Again, I warn every man: If you allow yourselves to be circumcised, you must follow all the law. ⁴If you try to be made right with God through the law, your life with Christ is over—you have left God's grace. ⁵But we have the true hope that comes from being made right with God, and by the Spirit we wait eagerly for this hope. ⁶When we are in Christ Jesus, it is not important if we are circumcised or not. The important thing is faith—the kind of faith that works through love.

⁷You were running a good race. Who stopped you from following the true way? ⁸This change did not come from the One who chose you. ⁹Be careful! "Just a little yeast makes the whole batch of dough rise." ¹⁰But I trust in the Lord that you will not believe those different ideas. Whoever is confusing you with such ideas will be punished.

¹¹My brothers and sisters, I do not teach that a man must be circumcised. If I teach circumcision, why am I still being attacked? If I still taught circumcision, my preaching about the cross would not be a problem. ¹²I wish the people who are bothering you would castrate themselves!

¹³My brothers and sisters, God called you to be free, but do not use your freedom as an excuse to do what pleases your sinful self. Serve each other with love. ¹⁴The whole law is made complete in this one command: "Love your neighbor as you love yourself." ¹⁵If you go on hurting each other and tearing each other apart, be careful, or you will completely destroy each other.

NKJV

²Indeed I, Paul, say to you that if you become circumcised, Christ will profit you nothing. ³And I testify again to every man who becomes circumcised that he is a debtor to keep the whole law. ⁴You have become estranged from Christ, you who attempt to be justified by law; you have fallen from grace. ⁵For we through the Spirit eagerly wait for the hope of righteousness by faith. ⁶For in Christ Jesus neither circumcision nor uncircumcision avails anything, but faith working through love.

⁷You ran well. Who hindered you from obeying the truth? ⁸This persuasion does not come from Him who calls you. ⁹A little leaven leavens the whole lump. ¹⁰I have confidence in you, in the Lord, that you will have no other mind; but he who troubles you shall bear his judgment, whoever he is.

¹¹And I, brethren, if I still preach circumcision, why do I still suffer persecution? Then the offense of the cross has ceased. ¹²I could wish that those who trouble you would even cut themselves off!

¹³For you, brethren, have been called to liberty; only do not use liberty as an opportunity for the flesh, but through love serve one another. ¹⁴For all the law is fulfilled in one word, even in this: "You shall love your neighbor as yourself." ¹⁵But if you bite and devour one another, beware lest you be consumed by one another!

EXPLORATION

1. Apparently some of the non-Jewish believers in Christ in Galatia were submitting to the Jewish rite of circumcision. Why?

2. What is the point behind religious rituals like baptism and the Lord's Supper?

3. Why are the ideas we embrace (or don't embrace) so important?

4. What's the acid test for whether our faith pleases God (v. 6)?

5. What does Paul say in this passage to suggest that the spiritual life is not about rule keeping but about relationship building?

INSPIRATION

True humility is not thinking lowly of yourself but thinking accurately of yourself. The humble heart does not say, "I can't do anything." But rather, "I can't do everything. I know my part and am happy to do it."

When Paul writes "*consider* others better than yourselves" (Phil. 2:3 NIV, emphasis mine), he uses a verb that means "to calculate," "to reckon." The word implies a conscious judgment resting on carefully weighed facts (Gerald F. Hawthorne, *Philippians,* vol. 43 of *Word Biblical Commentary* [Waco, TX: Word Publishing, 1983], 70). To consider others better than yourself, then, is not to say you have no place; it is to say that you know your place. "Don't cherish exaggerated ideas of yourself or your importance, but try to have a sane estimate of your capabilities by the light of the faith that God has given to you" (Rom. 12:3 PHILLIPS) . . .

Again, is Jesus not our example? Content to be known as a carpenter. Happy to be mistaken for the gardener. He served his followers by washing their feet. He serves us by doing the same. Each morning he gifts us with beauty. Each Sunday he calls us to his table. Each moment he dwells in our hearts. And does he not speak of the day when he as "the master will dress himself to serve and tell the servants to sit at the table, and he will serve them" (Luke 12:37 NCV)?

If Jesus is so willing to honor us, can we not do the same for others? Make people a priority. Accept your part in his plan . . . And, most of all, regard others as more important than yourself. Love does. For love "does not boast, it is not proud" (1 Cor. 13:4 NIV). (From *A Love Worth Giving* by Max Lucado)

REACTION

6. Why is the simple job description "Serve each other with love" (v. 13 NCV) so hard to live out?

7. How can a Christian tell when he or she is living by grace?

8. What does it mean to abuse grace?

9. What precautions should be taken to make sure that we don't misuse our freedom in Christ?

10. What are the likely problems in a fellowship that focuses on rule keeping? (Hint: see verses 13–15.)

11. Pick three people you will be encountering over the next forty-eight hours and list two specific ways you will commit to serve each one with love.

LIFE LESSONS

Christian freedom doesn't mean permission to do whatever. It means liberation from the prison of self-absorption and from enslavement to insecurity and pride. We grasp that God, in Christ, really does love us and accept us. We realize he lives in us to change us, to meet our needs, to touch others through us, and we are changed. We no longer have to strive to get his attention or earn his approval or stay in his good graces. We already enjoy those things to an infinite degree! Suddenly we are emancipated to turn our focus and attention to the needs of others. We serve them by letting divine love flow through us! The secret to a life of freedom? Resting in his perfect grace and relying on his infinite strength.

DEVOTION

Lord, open my eyes to the life-changing truth that "the important thing is faith—the kind of faith that works through love" (v. 6 NCV). Give me a heart to serve others with love.

For more Bible passages on being liberated and called to serve, see Matthew 20:28; Mark 10:43–44; Luke 10:25–37; John 13:14; Acts 20:18–19; Ephesians 6:7; and Philippians 2:1–8.

To complete the book of Galatians during this twelve-part study, read Galatians 5:2–15.

JOURNALING

What are the primary ways you've been gifted by God to serve others?

FOLLOWING THE SPIRIT

MAX
LUCADO

REFLECTION

It's popular today to speak of "spirituality." And yet often the word is typically used in vague and fuzzy ways that make no mention of God's Spirit. How would you explain the Spirit of God to a ten-year-old kid?

SITUATION

The Galatian letter argues that there are only two approaches to God. One is man-centered—calling on people to do certain things to merit God's approval. This way, Paul insists, is an exercise in futility. The other way is the good news that acceptance with God is possible because of what Jesus has already done for sinners. What's more, those who embrace this gospel receive God's Spirit to enable them to live a new kind of life.

OBSERVATION

Read Galatians 5:16–26 from the NCV or the NKJV.

NCV

¹⁶So I tell you: Live by following the Spirit. Then you will not do what your sinful selves want. ¹⁷Our sinful selves want what is against the Spirit, and the Spirit wants what is against our sinful selves. The two are against each other, so you cannot do just what you please. ¹⁸But if the Spirit is leading you, you are not under the law.

¹⁹The wrong things the sinful self does are clear: being sexually unfaithful, not being pure, taking part in sexual sins, ²⁰worshiping gods, doing witchcraft, hating, making trouble, being jealous, being angry, being selfish, making people angry with each other, causing divisions among people, ²¹feeling envy, being drunk, having wild and wasteful parties, and doing other things like these. I warn you now as I warned you before: Those who do these things will not inherit God's kingdom. ²²But the Spirit produces the fruit of love, joy, peace, patience, kindness, goodness, faithfulness, ²³gentleness, self-control. There is no law that says these things are wrong. ²⁴Those who belong to Christ Jesus have crucified their own sinful selves. They have given up their old selfish feelings and the evil things they wanted to do. ²⁵We get our new life from the Spirit, so we should follow the Spirit. ²⁶We must not be proud or make trouble with each other or be jealous of each other.

NKJV

¹⁶I say then: Walk in the Spirit, and you shall not fulfill the lust of the flesh. ¹⁷For the flesh lusts against the Spirit, and the Spirit against the flesh; and these are contrary to one another, so that you do not do the things that you wish. ¹⁸But if you are led by the Spirit, you are not under the law.

¹⁹Now the works of the flesh are evident, which are: adultery, fornication, uncleanness, lewdness, ²⁰idolatry, sorcery, hatred, contentions, jealousies, outbursts of wrath, selfish ambitions, dissensions, heresies, ²¹envy, murders, drunkenness, revelries, and the like; of which I tell you beforehand, just as I also told you in time past, that those who practice such things will not inherit the kingdom of God.

²²But the fruit of the Spirit is love, joy, peace, longsuffering, kindness, goodness, faithfulness, ²³gentleness, self-control. Against such there is no law. ²⁴And those who are Christ's have crucified the flesh with its passions and desires. ²⁵If we live in the Spirit, let us also walk in the Spirit. ²⁶Let us not become conceited, provoking one another, envying one another.

EXPLORATION

1. What does verse 17 mean when it speaks of our "flesh" (NKJV) or our "sinful selves" (NCV)?

2. How can a person tell when he or she is being led by the Spirit?

3. What do you make of the fact that in Paul's listing of various sins, he lumps selfishness and envy with "doing witchcraft" (v. 20 NCV) and "adultery" (v. 19 NKJV)?

4. What does it mean that those "who belong to Christ Jesus have crucified their own sinful selves" (v. 24 NCV)?

5. What counsel (using this passage) would you give to a Christian friend who admitted great impatience with a coworker?

INSPIRATION

Most Christians find the cross of Christ easier to accept than the Spirit of Christ. Good Friday makes more sense than Pentecost. Christ, our substitute. Jesus taking our place. The Savior paying for our sins. These are astounding, yet embraceable, concepts. They fall in the arena of transaction and substitution, familiar territory for us. But Holy Spirit discussions lead us into the realm of the supernatural and unseen. We grow quickly quiet and cautious, fearing what we can't see or explain.

It helps to consider the Spirit's work from this angle. What Jesus did in Galilee is what the Holy Spirit does in us. Jesus *dwelt among* the people, teaching, comforting, and convicting. The Holy Spirit *dwells within* us, teaching, comforting, and convicting. The preferred New Testament word for this promise is *oíkeo*, which means "live or dwell." *Oíkeo* descends from the Greek noun *oíkos*, which means "house." The Holy Spirit indwells the believer in the same way a homeowner indwells a house.

Those who trust God's actions in them find that God's Spirit is in them—living and breathing God! . . .

But if God himself has taken up residence in your life, you can hardly be thinking more of yourself than of him. Anyone, of course, who has not welcomed this invisible but clearly present God, the Spirit of Christ, won't know what we're talking about. But for you who welcome him, in whom he dwells—even though you still experience all the limitations of sin—you yourself experience life on God's terms (Rom. 8:5, 9–10 MSG). (*From* Come Thirsty *by Max Lucado*)

REACTION

6. Is it hard for you to grasp the biblical idea that God himself has taken up residence in your life, in the person of the Spirit of Christ?

7. The Spirit of God, when given free reign in our lives, produces various kinds of fruit (i.e., character qualities). Which of these qualities do you see growing in you?

8. We are told to follow the Spirit (v. 25), but how do we learn to hear his voice?

9. What inward spiritual struggles are you battling right now?

10. What would you tell a Christian friend who admitted one of the sinful acts or habits cited in Galatians 5:19–21?

11. How much and how often do you struggle with conceit and envy?

LIFE LESSONS

The Christian life isn't merely difficult; it's impossible. Impossible, that is, so long as we try to live for God in our own strength. Resisting sinful urges? Overcoming our natural tendencies toward pride and selfishness? Serving others in love? Face it—we will *never* do those things until we are surrendered to the Spirit of God. What a tragic mistake—and a devilish lie—to believe that we need the Spirit to begin the Christian life, but not to continue living it. Like a strong wind (John 3), like a mighty river (John 7), the Holy Spirit longs to move powerfully through each believer's soul. Revealing. Convicting. Comforting. Counseling. Teaching. Guiding. Transforming. Empowering. Have you invited him to do his work? Are you yielded fully to his leadership?

DEVOTION

Spirit of God, be unleashed in my heart. Do the work that only you can do. Fall fresh on me. Fill me. Mold me. Make me. Use me. Produce the character of Jesus in my life.

For more Bible passages on living in the Spirit, see Joel 2:28; Luke 24:49; John 14:17; 15:26; 16:13; Acts 1:8; Romans 8:9; and 1 Corinthians 3:16.

To complete the book of Galatians during this twelve-part study, read Galatians 5:16–26.

JOURNALING

What specific steps does a Christian need to take when encountering the desires of the old nature?

A GRACE-FULL LIFE

MAX LUCADO

REFLECTION

In a culture that champions the ideas of "live and let live" and "don't ask, don't tell" Christians tend to shy away from confronting one another when we engage in less-than-honorable activities. However, the Bible calls on believers to hold each other accountable. What has been your experience in this area? Have you ever been approached by another believer about your behavior? What happened?

SITUATION

Paul concludes that trying to live by the Old Testament Jewish law prompts proud people to compare and compete. Embracing grace results in Christians becoming a compassionate spiritual family. His final counsel to the Galatians? Stop worrying about how others are living and live like the new grace-filled people you are.

OBSERVATION

Read Galatians 6:1–18 from the NCV or the NKJV.

NCV

¹Brothers and sisters, if someone in your group does something wrong, you who are spiritual should go to that person and gently help make him right again. But be careful, because you might be tempted to sin, too. ²By helping each other with your troubles, you truly obey the law of Christ. ³If anyone thinks he is important when he really is not, he is only fooling himself. ⁴Each person should judge his own actions and not compare himself with others. Then he can be proud for what he himself has done. ⁵Each person must be responsible for himself.

⁶Anyone who is learning the teaching of God should share all the good things he has with his teacher. ⁷Do not be fooled: You cannot cheat God. People harvest only what they plant. ⁸If they plant to satisfy their sinful selves, their sinful selves will bring them ruin. But if they plant to please the Spirit, they will receive eternal life from the Spirit. ⁹We must not become tired of doing good. We will receive our harvest of eternal life at the right time if we do not give up. ¹⁰When we have the opportunity to help anyone, we should do it. But we should give special attention to those who are in the family of believers.

11See what large letters I use to write this myself. 12Some people are trying to force you to be circumcised so the Jews will accept them. They are afraid they will be attacked if they follow only the cross of Christ. 13Those who are circumcised do not obey the law themselves, but they want you to be circumcised so they can brag about what they forced you to do. 14I hope I will never brag about things like that. The cross of our Lord Jesus Christ is my only reason for bragging. Through the cross of Jesus my world was crucified, and I died to the world. 15It is not important if a man is circumcised or uncircumcised. The important thing is being the new people God has made. 16Peace and mercy to those who follow this rule—and to all of God's people.

17So do not give me any more trouble. I have scars on my body that show I belong to Christ Jesus.

18My brothers and sisters, the grace of our Lord Jesus Christ be with your spirit. Amen.

NKJV

1Brethren, if a man is overtaken in any trespass, you who are spiritual restore such a one in a spirit of gentleness, considering yourself lest you also be tempted. 2Bear one another's burdens, and so fulfill the law of Christ. 3For if anyone thinks himself to be something, when he is nothing, he deceives himself. 4But let each one examine his own work, and then he will have rejoicing in himself alone, and not in another. 5For each one shall bear his own load.

6Let him who is taught the word share in all good things with him who teaches.

7Do not be deceived, God is not mocked; for whatever a man sows, that he will also reap. 8For he who sows to his flesh will of the flesh reap corruption, but he who sows to the Spirit will of the Spirit reap everlasting life. 9And let us not grow weary while doing good, for in due season we shall reap if we do not lose heart. 10Therefore, as we have opportunity, let us do good to all, especially to those who are of the household of faith.

11See with what large letters I have written to you with my own hand! 12As many as desire to make a good showing in the flesh, these would compel you to be circumcised, only that they may not suffer persecution for the cross of Christ. 13For not even those who are circumcised keep the law, but they desire to have you circumcised that they may boast in your flesh. 14But God forbid that I should boast except in the cross of our Lord Jesus Christ, by whom the world has been crucified to me, and I to the world. 15For in Christ Jesus neither circumcision nor uncircumcision avails anything, but a new creation.

16And as many as walk according to this rule, peace and mercy be upon them, and upon the Israel of God.

17From now on let no one trouble me, for I bear in my body the marks of the Lord Jesus.

18Brethren, the grace of our Lord Jesus Christ be with your spirit. Amen.

EXPLORATION

1. What is the right response when a fellow believer succumbs to temptation?

2. How does one decide whether it is appropriate to confront another person?

3. Why is conceit so dangerous?

4. Describe the spiritual law that "we reap what we sow."

5. How does an increasing confidence in the cross of Christ demonstrate growth?

INSPIRATION

I like the story of the little boy who fell out of bed. When his Mom asked him what happened, he answered, "I don't know. I guess I stayed too close to where I got in."

Easy to do the same with our faith. It's tempting just to stay where we got in and never move.

Pick a time in the not-too-distant past. A year or two ago. Now ask yourself a few questions. How does your prayer life today compare with then? How about your giving? Have both the amount and the joy increased? What about your church loyalty? Can you tell you've grown? And Bible study? Are you learning to learn?

We will in all things **grow up** *into him who is the Head, that is, Christ.* (Eph. 4:15 NIV, emphasis mine)

Let us leave the elementary teachings about Christ and go on to **maturity.** (Heb. 6:1 NIV, emphasis mine)

Like newborn babies, crave pure spiritual milk, so that by it you may **grow up** *in your salvation.* (1 Pet. 2:2 NIV, emphasis mine)

But grow in the grace and knowledge of our Lord and Savior Jesus Christ. (2 Pet. 3:18 NIV, emphasis mine)

Growth is the goal of the Christian. Maturity is mandatory. If a child ceased to develop, the parent would be concerned, right? Doctors would be called. Tests would be run. When a child stops growing, something is wrong.

When a Christian stops growing, help is needed. If you are the same Christian you were a few months ago, be careful. You might be wise to get a checkup. Not on your body, but on your heart. Not a physical, but a spiritual. (From *When God Whispers Your Name* by Max Lucado)

REACTION

6. Growth. Maturity. Life change. By whatever name you call it, how specifically have you grown in recent years?

7. Paul says that we are to "bear one another's burdens" (v. 2 NKJV) even as each one bears "his own load" (v. 5 NKJV). What's the difference?

8. How can we help our brothers and sisters grow out of a stagnant faith?

9. How does a Christian "do" verse 6? What does that look like?

10. How do you stay motivated to keep loving and serving others, especially on days when you feel like quitting?

11. As much as you can tell, what are some concrete opportunities you have in the next day or so to "do good to all, especially to those who are of the household of faith" (v. 10 NKJV)?

LIFE LESSONS

Paul sums up his timeless message to the Galatians in 6:15: "It is not important if a man is circumcised or uncircumcised. The important thing is being the new people God has made" (NCV). While few modern believers struggle with the issue of circumcision, we constantly battle other legalistic pressures. Always there is the temptation to fall back into a rule-keeping mind-set—that subtle, insidious way of thinking that says, "I must follow certain religious rules if I want God's approval." To this Paul says, "No! The spiritual life that pleases God (and satisfies our own souls) is being the new creatures that God has made us to be" (see 2 Corinthians 5:17). We live by grace. We grow by following the leading of God's Spirit, who lives in us. True spirituality isn't imposed from without; it bubbles up and overflows from within.

DEVOTION

Father, I want so much to know your grace, to revel in it, to be changed by it, to share it with the world. Keep me from pride. Cause me to realize that "the cross of our Lord Jesus Christ is my only reason for bragging" (v. 14 NCV).

For more Bible passages on living by grace, see Psalm 84:11; Acts 13:43; Luke 2:40; 2 Corinthians 8:9; 12:9; 2 Timothy 2:1; and 1 Peter 5:5.

To complete the book of Galatians during this twelve-part study, read Galatians 6:1–18.

JOURNALING

What does Paul mean when he writes, "Through the cross of Jesus my world was crucified, and I died to the world" (Gal. 6:14 NCV)?

Lucado Life Lesson Series

*Revised and updated, the Lucado Life Lessons series is perfect
for small group or individual use and includes intriguing questions
that will take you deeper into God's Word.*

THOMAS NELSON
Since 1798

Available at your local Christian Bookstore.